HAL•LEONARD®
MANDOLIN
PLAY-ALONG

AUDIO ACCESS INCLUDED

J.S. BACH

Page	Title
2	Bourrée in E Minor
4	Invention No. 1
6	Invention No. 2
8	Jesu, Joy of Man's Desiring
3	March in D Major
10	Minuet in G
12	Musette in D Major
14	Sleepers, Awake (Wachet Auf)

PLAYBACK+
Speed • Pitch • Balance • Loop

To access audio visit:
www.halleonard.com/mylibrary

6739-4705-5218-4350

Mandolin arranged and recorded by Mike Cramer

ISBN 978-1-4584-1388-8

7777 W. BLUEMOUND RD. P.O. BOX 13819 MILWAUKEE, WI 53213

In Australia Contact:
Hal Leonard Australia Pty. Ltd.
4 Lentara Court
Cheltenham, Victoria, 3192 Australia
Email: ausadmin@halleonard.com.au

Visit Hal Leonard Online at
www.halleonard.com

T0050635

Bourrée in E Minor

By Johann Sebastian Bach

March in D Major

By Johann Sebastian Bach

Moderately slow, in 2 ♩ = 90

Invention No. 1

By Johann Sebastian Bach

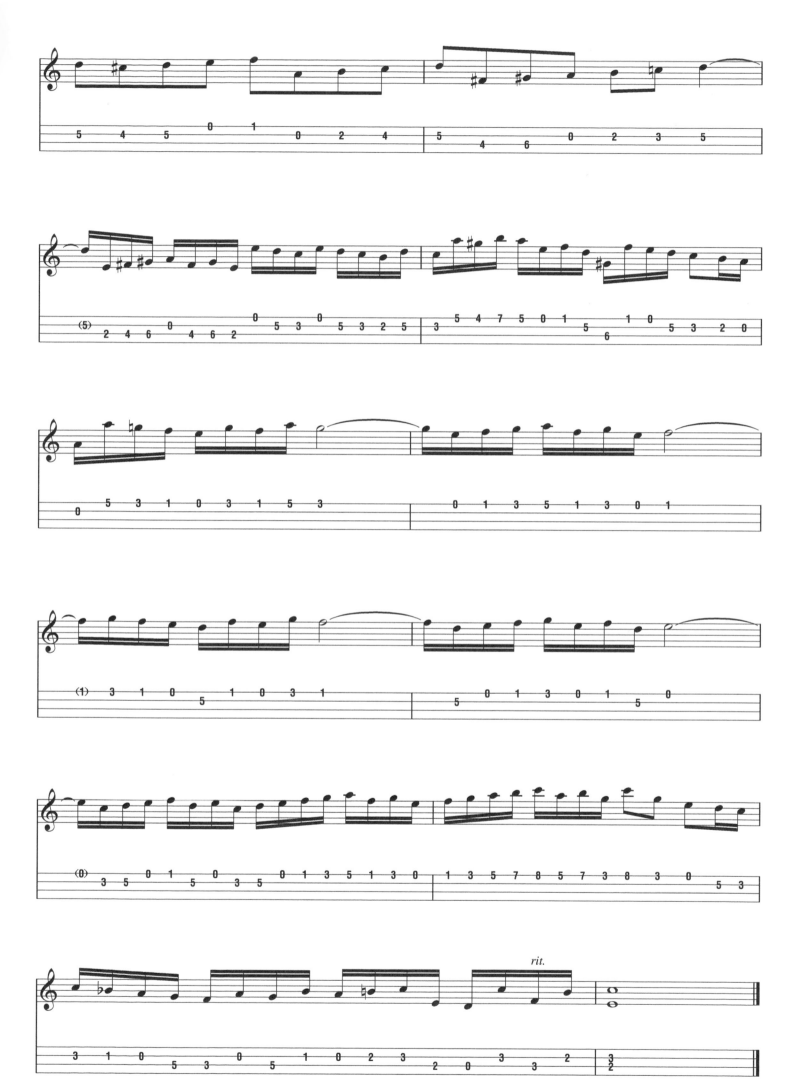

Invention No. 2

By Johann Sebastian Bach

Slow ♩ = 60

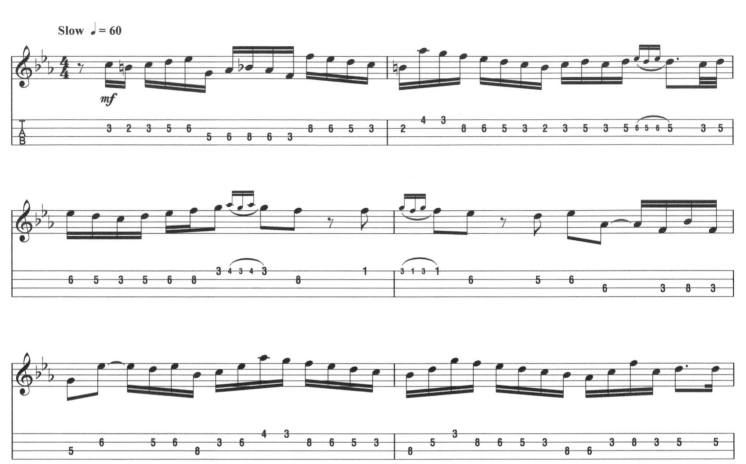

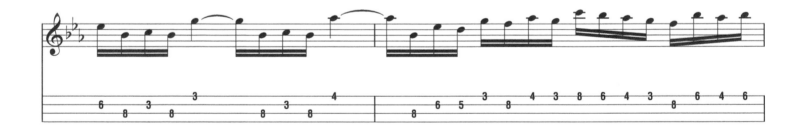

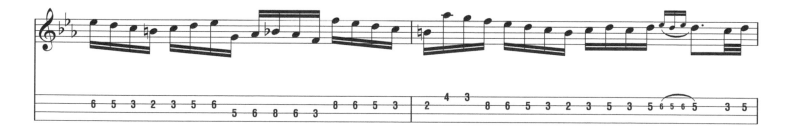

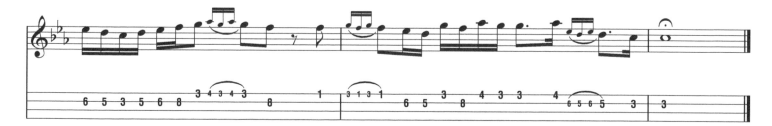

Jesu, Joy of Man's Desiring

By Johann Sebastian Bach

Slow ♩. = 66

9

Minuet in G

By Johann Sebastian Bach

Musette in D Major

By Johann Sebastian Bach

Sleepers, Awake
(Wachet Auf)
By Johann Sebastian Bach

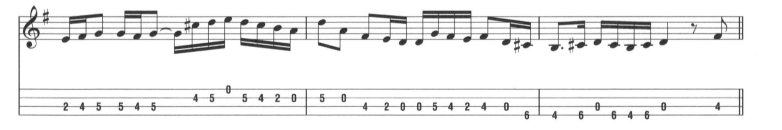